A FLORENTINE MERCHANT

PETER BEDRICK BOOKS
New York

Contents

Introduction

This story is about Zita, a young slave girl who lived in Prato, a small town near Florence in Italy, during the late fourteenth century AD. She had been born in a village in southern Russia, but had been captured by bandits when she was about 12 years old and sold into slavery.

Many wealthy people in Italy kept slaves at that time. The Church did not allow Christian people to be bought and sold as slaves, but did permit Christians to buy and sell people of other faiths as slaves. Most people in the area where Zita came from were Muslims, although a few still followed the beliefs of their ancestors.

The household in Prato where Zita lived belonged to Messer Francesco, a rich merchant. The house is still standing today, and can be visited. We know a great deal about life in this house because Messer Francesco wrote thousands of letters about his business and household affairs, and kept many books of accounts as well. We can read all these today and learn how the house was built, what food was cooked and eaten, how Messer Francesco's business was prospering and even what happened to his family and servants when a dreadful plague infected and killed many people living in Prato.

This book tells the story of two years in the life of Zita and the people who lived with her in Messer Francesco's house. At the end of the book, you can see some detailed pictures of the house itself and some of its contents, and of Messer Francesco's country estate outside the town.

In the Kitchen

It was hot in the kitchen. Everyone seemed to be in a hurry. Zita, the slave girl, sighed.

'Why are we all so busy?' she asked.

'It's because Messer Francesco, your master, is coming home today,' replied Donna Margherita, 'and he expects to find an extra-special meal waiting for him when he arrives.'

Zita nodded. At last, she thought, she was getting used to life in this busy household.

A year ago, things had been very different. One day, when she was looking after her family's herd of goats, a gang of fierce bandits had galloped out of the woods. They had carried her away from her village in southern Russia to the great slave market in the city of Constantinople. There, she had been sold by the bandits to some Italian slave-traders, who had taken her on another terrible journey across the sea to the busy port of Venice. She had been crammed into a ship with crowds of other slaves. They had all been dreadfully sick. Zita had cried for her family. Most of the other slaves came from lands to the far south, and did not speak her language. But they had been kind, and had comforted her as well as they could.

In Venice, Messer Francesco's servants had bargained with the slave-traders, and had brought Zita home to Prato, the town in northern Italy where Messer Francesco lived.

Messer Francesco was a rich and successful merchant. He had many people to help him in his business. His wife, Donna Margherita, had slaves and servants to work for her in the house. Zita had felt lonely, but old Lucia, who had worked for Donna Margherita for many years, had made her feel welcome and had taught her to speak Italian.

Lucia bustled across the kitchen. 'Stop daydreaming, child,' she said kindly. Her voice made Zita jump. 'There's still a lot to do before Messer Francesco arrives.'

The New Picture

Zita had been sent with some of the servants to clear away all the furniture from the entrance hall of Messer Francesco's house. A famous artist would soon be coming to paint a large picture of St Christopher on the wall opposite the main door.

'The blessed saint will bring good luck to anyone who leaves on a journey,' explained Lucia. She knew all about the house, and could remember it being built. 'It took ten years,' she said, 'with our master fussing and criticizing all the time. You know how he always likes everything to be perfect. He nagged the workmen until he got exactly what he wanted. It will be the same with this painter, just you wait and see.'

Lucia was right. Messer Francesco had asked Maestro Niccolo Gerini to paint the picture. One day, in the street, Zita overheard Maestro Niccolo complaining to another artist.

'Yes, I'm working for that old miser Francesco Datini at the moment,' he had said. 'He always wants the finest materials, but he grumbles like anything about the bills.'

Messer Francesco had employed many skilful artists and craftsmen to build and decorate his house. Now the rooms were covered with bright patterns, all beautifully painted on the smooth plaster surface of each wall. When Zita had first arrived in Prato, she had been dazzled. But Lucia had told her that there were many finer houses in the great city of Florence.

'He likes to think he's top dog, here in his home town,' Lucia said, 'but there are many richer men in Florence. You should see some of the great nobles and their palaces there.'

'Maybe I will, one day,' replied Zita. 'But I'd rather see my home and family once more.'

'Now, now, don't get gloomy again,' said Lucia briskly. 'Come and help me clean the upstairs rooms. I'm glad we don't have a palace in Florence to look after. There's quite enough housework to do here in Prato!'

Hard Work

'I'm so tired!' Zita yawned, as she met Lucia in the upstairs corridor one morning. 'Donna Margherita looks very pale today, too. We slaves and servants have to work very hard; that's to be expected. But Messer Francesco expects poor Donna Margherita to work long hours as well. It's easy for him to sit in Florence giving out orders, but back here in Prato, it's she who has to organize everything.'

Zita yawned again, and went on, 'Do you know, she's up first in the morning to unlock the big front door, and then at night, she stays up after everyone else has gone to bed. She checks that all the doors and windows are closed, and that all of us are safe inside.'

'Don't you worry about her,' replied Lucia. 'She's very capable. I remember when she first came to live with Messer Francesco, just after they were married; she was only sixteen. She's learned such a lot since then! Now she knows all about cooking and gardening and how to keep the house running smoothly. Why, she couldn't even read and write, and now she has to organize the whole household and write reports on everything in her letters to Messer Francesco.'

Donna Margherita sometimes complained in her letters to Messer Francesco about the 'pack of useless women' she had to help her. So Messer Francesco expected her to watch over everything they did, from cooking the food, cleaning out the wine barrels, spinning and weaving linen cloth to caring for the children.

Donna Margherita had no children herself, but she looked after her little niece, Tina, and a very pretty girl, a few years older than Zita, called Ginevra. Lucia told Zita that Ginevra's mother had been a slave. 'But Messer Francesco is her father, so we must treat her with proper respect,' she said.

11

In the Marketplace

Zita always liked going shopping with Donna Margherita, even though it meant a heavy load to carry on the way back home.

The market was held in a big square in the center of Prato. The cloth merchants set up their stalls there. Buying and selling wool and cloth was the main trade of the town.

Donna Margherita and Zita threaded their way through the narrow streets to the market. It was noisy and crowded, but there was lots to see. All the shops had open fronts. In one, a cobbler sat mending shoes, laughing and joking with the passers-by. In another shop, Zita could see the apothecary. His mysterious jars of brilliantly-colored medicines were guaranteed to cure all ills. They stopped at the tailor's shop, where the master tailor and his apprentice were busy making a new cloak for Donna Margherita. She tried it on. It looked very fine.

'It will be ready next week, madam,' the tailor promised. 'We will deliver it to your house.'

Close by, they could hear the clink of coins from the money-changer's shop, as he weighed the fine gold florins in his delicately-balanced scales.

On their way home, they passed the stalls where the fishermen displayed their catch – eels, carp and pike. Donna Margherita pointed to some silvery carp heaped in a basket. 'We'll take some of those, please,' she said.

The fisherman handed the wrapped package of fish to Zita for her to carry. As they left the fish stall, Donna Margherita told Zita about the rules set out by the town council to make sure that only fresh food was sold in the market.

'If it's something that goes bad quickly in hot weather, like fish,' she explained, 'the council makes the merchants throw the unsold food away at the end of each day.'

'But isn't that a waste?' asked Zita.

'Oh no,' Donna Margherita replied. 'All the poor people rush to pick up the food that is being thrown away. They get a meal for free!'

The Mule Train

When Zita first arrived in Prato, she was puzzled to find that Messer Francesco spent very little time in his splendid new house. He always seemed to be away on business.

Lucia explained. 'Our master is a very busy merchant. He buys and sells goods all over Europe. Now he has opened a shop in Florence, where he sells goods to wealthy customers. He stays there for weeks at a time.'

Zita was used to seeing the mule trains which arrived almost every day at the house in Prato, laden with goods from Florence, letters for Donna Margherita, and even Messer Francesco's dirty laundry. Most days, the servants loaded up another mule train to make the return journey from Prato to Florence. The mules carried fresh fruit and vegetables from the garden in Prato or from the country estate near by, loaves of bread, eggs carefully packed in straw, basins of pork jelly made by Donna Margherita herself, and all sorts of other delicacies. Messer Francesco was very fond of good food.

One day, Zita was helping to unload the baskets from the mules when Ginevra called to her. 'Zita, come here a minute! I'd like you to help me with this.'

She was stirring an evil-looking mixture in a little dish over the fire.

'Whatever is it?' asked Zita, wrinkling up her nose at the smell.

'Don't look like that!' replied Ginevra. 'It's a new medicine for Donna Margherita. She's ill again, with another attack of malaria. You know how she suffers. An old peasant woman told her about this remedy. It's meant to drive away headaches. You stew a black pudding slowly in wine, and then strain off the liquid. When it's ready, you must come and help me bathe Donna Margherita's forehead with it. You know how kind she is to us. We must try to help her now she's ill.'

Messer Francesco at Work

One day, when Zita was helping to unload yet another mule train, she got talking to one of the mule drivers.

'What does Messer Francesco do all day in the big city of Florence?' she asked. 'How does he make all his money?'

Gano, the muledriver, shrugged his shoulders.

'I don't know how he makes his money, but I can tell you what he does all day, right enough. I've seen it with my own eyes! Writes! That's what he does. All day, and half the night too, sometimes. Nothing but letters, letters, letters.'

'But surely he is rich enough to employ someone to write his letters for him?' replied Zita.

'Of course he is,' said Gano. 'And he has partners who would be happy to help him run his business. But Messer Francesco is one of those who must do everything themselves. He insists that nobody can run the business as well as he can. He sits at his desk all day. Sometimes he is so busy that he doesn't have a meal until sunset, and even then he goes back to work by candlelight. He writes long letters every week to the managers of his branches in various cities throughout Italy, and in France, Majorca and Minorca as well.

'He gets very impatient if people make mistakes. Just the other day I heard him shouting at one of the clerks who help him. He went on and on. "You haven't the mind of a cat!"'

'I've seen the letters he sends to Donna Margherita,' said Zita. 'He's always fussing about details.'

'Yes, that's right!' agreed Gano. 'He's just as particular when he sends a letter, too. Each letter is fastened with string, and then wrapped in waterproof cloth. Sometimes I have to travel with letters for him. It can be dangerous – I've been attacked on my journeys before now. So Messer Francesco often sends more than one copy of a letter by different routes if it's really important that his message arrives.'

Travellers' Tales

All sorts of interesting people used to come to the house in Prato when Messer Francesco was at home. One day, as Zita came into the kitchen, she saw a tall, sunburnt stranger talking to Lucia and some of the other servants. His name was Marco and he made journeys overseas for Messer Francesco. He was telling Lucia about his last voyage to Majorca, off the coast of Italy.

'It wasn't a bad trip,' he was saying. 'We bought twenty-nine sacks of wool last May, straight after the sheep had been shorn. All good quality fleeces, mind you! Messer Francesco likes the best. Then we had to charter a ship to bring back the wool to Italy.'

He smiled round at his audience. Lucia filled his beaker once again with wine.

'Thank you kindly,' he said. 'Now, where was I? Ah yes, about to leave Majorca for the voyage home. Those waters can be very dangerous, you know, because of the Barbary pirates. They sail along the North African coast, waiting to attack any well-laden ship. The pirates are fierce and ruthless. There's nothing they like better than a slow merchant ship, with no soldiers aboard to defend her.

'The first part of the journey back wasn't too bad, though we had to keep a careful lookout. We travelled in convoy with several other ships. But after we left Barcelona, in Spain, for the second part of our journey, we were on our own. I had hired a dozen Spanish archers to defend us, just in case. And it was a good thing that I did, for we were threatened on our second day at sea. The archers put on a good display, and Fortune sent a sudden storm, which meant that the pirates couldn't sail towards us and overtake us. We spent a very anxious night, but by dawn our attackers had vanished. Maybe they had found a better prize to chase.'

He stopped to take another gulp of his wine.

'Mind you,' he added, 'there are dangers everywhere, on land just as much as at sea. You can be attacked by outlaws or bandits in broad daylight in some wild regions.'

'Yes, I know,' said Zita, thoughtfully.

At Avignon

The next time Messer Francesco came home to Prato from Florence, he brought his friend, the lawyer Ser Lapo Mazzei, to stay. One evening, the two of them settled down to enjoy a flask of local wine. Donna Margherita sent Zita along to pour the wine for them, and to fetch food for them if they felt hungry.

'Just you mind your manners, my girl, when you're in such important company,' she said.

Messer Francesco was telling Ser Lapo how he began his career as a merchant.

'It started when I was about fifteen,' he said. 'My father had left me a little bit of land here in Prato. It wasn't really enough to live on, and so I sold it. With that money in my pocket, I set off for Avignon in France. At that time, the popes lived in Avignon and not in Rome.

'It was a marvellous place to be. Thousands of people were crowded together in the town. Many of them were important church officials or high-ranking priests, and they all had lots of money to spend. All I had to do was to import luxury goods – silver, spices, fine cloth, perfumes – and I could sell them straight away. I sold some wool, too, but the best profits came from selling armor and weapons. At that time, there were armies fighting all over France, all keen to buy new armor, lances and swords.'

Ser Lapo chuckled. 'And, knowing you, I'm sure you didn't worry too much about who you sold the armor and weapons to!'

'My friend, how true!' replied Messer Francesco. There's always more profit in selling to both sides in a quarrel!'

'I suppose that was when you invented that motto of yours: "In the name of God and Profit",' said Ser Lapo, smiling.

'Quite right!' exclaimed Messer Francesco. 'I make sure that it's written on the first page of all my ledgers. It's a good motto. And it reminds those lazy clerks of mine that they must be honest and work hard for me to help make a profit.'

The Country Estate

'Zita, are you ready?' called Lucia.

Messer Francesco, Donna Margherita, Ginevra and several of their servants were getting ready for the journey to Messer Francesco's country estate. It stood on a wooded hillside near Prato, called Il Palco. The farm there had originally belonged to Donna Margherita's family, but now Messer Francesco owned it. Over the years he had bought land all around the old farmhouse and had started to build a new country house at Il Palco.

Whenever he had time to spare, Messer Francesco went out to the countryside to help the workmen with his own hands – and also to interfere with everything they did. He was always shouting, fussing and giving orders.

The new country house was very large and spacious, but bare and drab inside when compared with the richly-decorated house at Prato. There were granaries to store wheat and barley, and cellars to keep the barrels of wine and olive oil cool and fresh.

As well as olives and grapes, the farm produced eggs, chickens, ducks, pigeons and lots of vegetables. Zita sighed. She knew that in the months to come she would spend a lot of her time packing up this farm produce to send to her master in Florence. 'But at least,' she thought, 'I will eat some of it in the kitchen in Prato!'

On the journey back to Prato, Lucia told Zita how one year there had been a great panic when a band of rough soldiers had rampaged through the countryside, stealing cows and horses and burning down houses and farms.

'Messer Francesco heard that this wild army was on the move, so he brought all his farmworkers and their families into Prato where they would be safe.' Lucia went on, 'Needless to say, he organized all this from Florence. He sent all his orders by letter to poor Donna Margherita, and she had to try to carry them out. But she managed very well, and everyone reached Prato in safety.'

Plague!

All summer there had been rumors and, by August, the dreadful truth was clear: the plague had come to Prato! It was a dreadful disease which killed many of its victims within days.

'It is sent by God,' said Lucia, 'to punish us for our sins. Say your prayers, Zita, and you, too, Ginevra! We never know when death will strike!'

'Now, now, Lucia,' said Donna Margherita, coming into the room. 'Don't give up hope so easily. Messer Francesco has decided that we should all go to join him in Florence. There's no plague there, yet. By all means say your prayers, but come and help me pack up, too!'

When they reached Florence, they found the people there every bit as worried and fearful as the citizens of Prato had been. They flocked to the preachers who called on them to pray for God's forgiveness for their sins; many made promises of great gifts to the church or to the poor if only the city could be kept free of the disease.

Messer Francesco decided to go on a pilgrimage. He set out one morning with eleven other men – two business partners, eight of his workmen and his brother-in-law. They dressed themselves in long white robes to show that they were sorry for their past sins. Some of them carried little whips.

'They will hit themselves around the neck and shoulders with them,' explained Lucia. 'They make themselves suffer pain to punish themselves for any wrong they have done in the past.'

The twelve men first attended a service at a nearby church, and then they joined a huge crowd of thousands of others, all barefoot and clothed in white. They took food with them, and warm clothes to wear at night. After nine long days they returned home to Florence.

The pilgrimage did not work. The plague came to Florence after all. Hundreds of people died. Eventually, Messer Francesco moved his entire household to the distant town of Bologna. It was over a year before they dared return to Florence or to their home in Prato.

25

Ginevra's Wedding

One morning, not long after their return to Prato, Donna Margherita came bustling in. She was very excited. Ginevra followed her, looking happy and rather nervous, all at the same time.

'What is it, madam?' asked Lucia. 'Do you have some special news today?'

'Oh yes, I do!' replied Donna Margherita, rather breathlessly. 'Great news! Ginevra is to be married, and to a rich young man called Lionardo! Messer Francesco tells me that after six years of bargaining, he has agreed with Lionardo's cousin – that's his business partner, you remember him, don't you? – on the terms for a marriage agreement between our family and his. It's very important that Ginevra marries a rich and hard-working young man. They will have to carry on the family business and keep up the family's good name when Messer Francesco and I are dead and gone.'

'Does Ginevra like this Lionardo?' asked Zita, when Donna Margherita and Ginevra had left the room.

'Well, she hardly knows him,' replied Lucia. 'He was chosen for her some time ago by Donna Margherita and Messer Francesco. In this country, young girls have to obey their family's wishes.'

The wedding was a splendid occasion. Zita was pleased to see that Ginevra did look happy, after all. Lionardo was a kindly young man. After the wedding feast, there was much laughing and joking when Donna Margherita made Ginevra hold a baby in her arms. It was the infant daughter of one of her friends. One of the servants rushed across to place a gold coin in Ginevra's shoe, as well.

'Why are they doing that?' asked Zita.

'It's to show that we wish them good fortune and many children,' Lucia explained.

'And a long and happy life, too!' added Zita. 'Goodbye, Ginevra, I shall miss you!'

Picture Glossary

Left: Coat of arms of the Prato wool merchants' guild

The house at Prato

Messer Francesco's house in Prato was built around a courtyard, which had a well in the center. It also had a garden. These were luxuries, since land for building was very scarce and expensive in Prato. Most people lived in cramped houses without gardens, and had to make do with water carried from the town's public fountains.

Francesco also had a warehouse and office built behind the new house. He never liked to be too far away from his work!

Right: Farming tools

1 plowshare
2 plow
3 hoe
4 foot-rest spade
5 two-pronged hoe
6 pruning hook

Messer Francesco also built a large house in the country, called 'Il Palco'. He employed laborers to grow grain, fruit and vegetables to feed his family and servants, and also for sale.

Inside the house there was a loggia, an open area rather like a balcony, on each floor. This let light and air into the rooms, and was used for entertaining. The main kitchen was on the first floor, a custom which survived from the days before chimneys, when smoke had to escape through a hole in the roof.

Right: Messer Francesco's coat of arms

Key to ground-floor plan (below right)

1   storeroom
2   stable
3   warehouse office
4   garden
5   kitchen
6   dining room
7   storeroom
8   courtyard
9   reception hall
10 spare bedroom
11 Messer Francesco's office

Il Palco

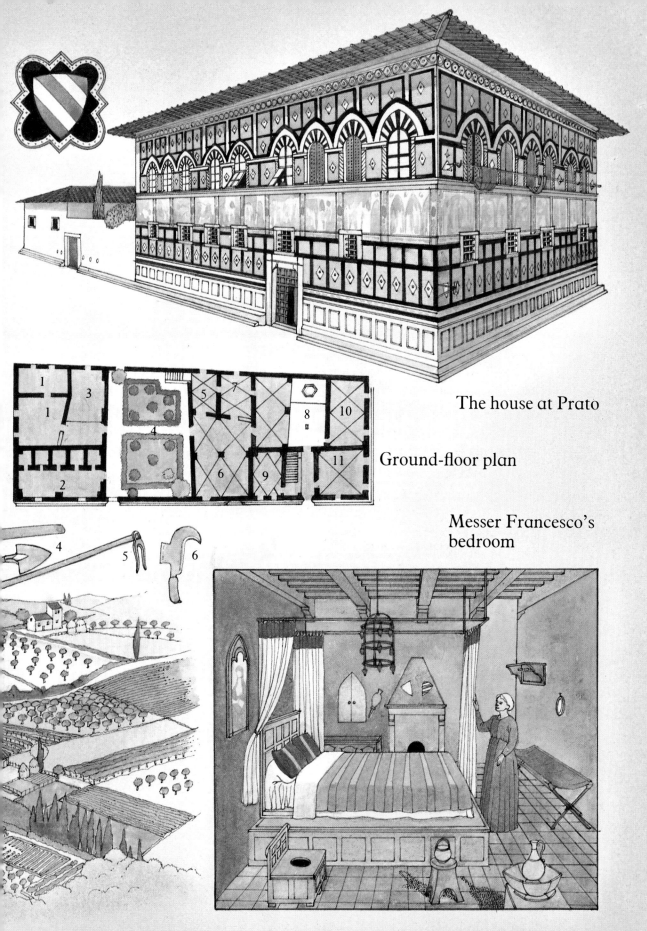

The house at Prato

Ground-floor plan

Messer Francesco's
bedroom

Finding Out More

Books to Read

When Messer Francesco died, he left all his letters and papers to his home town of Prato. They have survived there for over 500 years, and were used to write a very famous book, called **The Merchant of Prato**. It was written by Iris Origo, and has appeared in several different versions. You should be able to find it in most public libraries. It is a book for adults, so you may need someone to help you with it, but it contains many fascinating quotations from Messer Francesco's letters and papers. Other books about medieval Europe you might like to read are:

G. Caselli **The Renaissance and New World** Peter Bedrick Books 1986

M. Lodge **The Open Book of Medieval Times** Hodder and Stoughton 1981

F. Macdonald **The Middle Ages** Macdonald Educational 1984

A. Powell **Renaissance Italy** (Great Civilisations Series) Longman 1979

G. Thie **Living in the Past, The Middle Ages** Basil Blackwell 1983